Ludwig
BEETHOVEN
And the Chiming Tower Bells

By
OPAL WHEELER

Illustrated by Mary Greenwalt

Zeezok
PUBLISHING

Ludwig Beethoven and the Chiming Tower Bells
Written by Opal Wheeler

LUDWIG BEETHOVEN AND THE CHIMING TOWER BELLS written by Opal Wheeler. Copyright © 1944 by E.P. Dutton & Co., Inc. Copyright renewed © 1972 by Opal Wheeler. Published by arrangement with Dutton Children's Books, a division of Penguin Young Readers Group, a member of Penguin Group (USA) Inc.

ISBN 978-0-9746505-6-2
Republished November, 2007
Printed in the United States of America

Zeezok Publishing, LLC
PO Box 1960 • Elyria, OH 44036
info@Zeezok.com • 1-800-749-1681

www.Zeezok.com

MUSIC

LUDWIG BEETHOVEN
And the Chiming Tower Bells

CHAPTER ONE

The good folk of the quaint little city of Bonn hurried into their tall pointed houses and locked the doors tightly against the bitter December thunder-storm that suddenly beat down upon them from the Seven Mountains.

The icy wind tore at the shutters and howled in the chimneys, racing on through the valley of the Rhine to churn the waters of the old river into foam and toss the ferry boat on the high white-capped waves.

Grandfather Beethoven stood on deck with the captain, his old red coat pulled close around his broad shoulders against the driving rain.

"A bad night ahead, Captain."

"Aye, and not another crossing for us this day."

Soon the struggling ferry was landed at the wide pier of Bonn, nestling safely at the foothills of the mountains.

Grandfather Beethoven stepped ashore and tramped through the wet cobbled streets, stopping now and then to look in the windows of his good neighbors, gathered snugly around their crackling hearth fires.

The Bonngasse at last! Opening the low green gate, he crossed the small garden and slowly climbed the long back stairs to the attic rooms at the top.

How cold it was in the poor, three-roomed home of his son! As he softly closed the door, a flash of lightning made the tiny bedroom as bright as day. A crash of thunder shook the walls and a baby cried lustily in the dark.

"Ah, my good Maria, the little one is here!"

"Yes, Grandfather, and you will see what a fine boy he is, too!" answered Mother Beethoven softly.

Lighting a candle, Grandfather Louis bent over the old worn bed and looked for a long time at his new grandson.

"He is not a pretty baby, Maria, but he makes a good noise! Perhaps he will be a fine singer some day, like his Grandfather!"

As the thunder growled and the wind and rain beat through the cracks in the window, the wailing grew louder than ever.

"There, there, my little one, do not cry so," crooned Mother Beethoven tucking the coverlet closer around the small baby.

Grandfather Beethoven hurried to his home across the street, and was soon climbing the stairs again, his arms piled high with wood.

Before long, the fires were blazing cheerily, and the new baby, warm at last, fell fast asleep beside his mother.

Early the next morning, Father Beethoven carried his new son to the cold stone church of St. Remigius near by, where he was christened Ludwig van Beethoven.

In the months that went quickly by, little Ludwig heard music much of the time, for Father Beethoven was a singer in the royal choir at the Elector's palace, and gave lessons on the violin and piano to the children of noble families.

And there were many concerts in the low attic rooms, when the neighbors of the Bonngasse

gathered together to play on their instruments with Father Beethoven until far into the night.

But the best time of all was in the early morning, when Grandfather Beethoven came to visit his small grandson.

"Sing! Sing!" called the brown-skinned, black-haired little Ludwig. As Grandfather Louis, in his deep voice, began the songs that he had sung so many years ago in the royal choir, the small boy waved his arms in time to the singing.

"Just see the child, Johann — he does not miss a single beat!"

"Yes, Father. Perhaps he, too, will become a musician, like all the Beethovens!"

As soon as Ludwig was old enough to run about on his short, stocky legs, he was seldom at home, for every morning, almost as soon as he opened his big black eyes, he ran across the street to look for Grandfather Beethoven.

"Ludwig! So early you are, little one — just like the sparrows!"

After they had eaten their simple meal of sausage and bread, they wandered happily together through the busy market square and on back to the narrow Bonngasse, to chat with their good neighbors along the way.

Always there was music, for almost everyone along the cobbled street played on an instrument, and Ludwig's dark eyes grew wide with wonder as Herr Ries gently drew the bow across the strings of his violin, or Simrock blew into his long golden horn, the lovely melodies filling all the sunlit air.

In the springtime, there were long walks beyond the old city walls, when Ludwig ran happily about in the sweet-smelling meadows. When he grew tired, Grandfather Beethoven swung him high onto his broad shoulder and sang him songs of long ago, his deep voice ringing out through the wide valley.

And there were stories of the time when he had journeyed all the way from his home in Holland, to earn his living as a choir boy in the little city of Bonn, and there, at last, he had become the well-known Kappelmeister, loved by everyone, far and near.

Ludwig loved the days with his grandfather, who was always so kind and took such good care of him. But the happy times could not go on, for one day Grandfather Beethoven died.

Ludwig was very lonely now, and sadly missed his gentle companion more and more as the days went slowly by.

And there were times when he was cold and hungry, for Grandfather Louis was no longer there to bring him food to eat, and fuel to keep the fires burning brightly.

Before going to his work each morning, Father Beethoven sat to play at the old worn piano, while Ludwig stood close by, watching his flying fingers and listening eagerly to the beautiful sounds.

Father Beethoven looked down at the small boy, standing there so still.

"Come, my son, now it is time to see what you can do with music," and lifting the four-year-old Ludwig to

his knees, he watched quietly as the short fingers pressed down the keys very gently, picking out a little melody that he had just heard.

Father Beethoven was delighted.

"Yes, yes! It is time for us to work together, my child. And when you can play well, you will give a fine concert, like the boy, Mozart, and bring us much money, and costly presents, as well."

Ludwig learned very quickly, and Father Beethoven was proud, indeed, when the little boy was able to play the difficult accompaniments of his songs, while he sang the solos in his high tenor voice.

The neighbors, gathered around the piano, listened in amazement.

"Bravo! Bravo, little musician! Surely he will be another Mozart some day!"

And now there were lessons on the violin, as well. Ludwig liked to work with Father Beethoven, but when the pieces became more difficult, and the hours of practicing were longer, he grew very weary.

"I will learn to play when I am older, Father."

"No, my son — now is the good time to study music."

Sometimes Ludwig played in the garden below with the neighbor children, but he could never stay for long, for always there was the practicing to be done.

Mother Beethoven watched sadly as the small boy stood on a low stool before the piano, playing difficult scales and exercises hour after hour, or drawing the bow across the strings of his small violin until the tones were sweet and true.

"Ah, my little one, it is enough now. There is the water to get, for soon your father will be here, and no supper ready."

"I will draw it for you, Mother!" cried the delighted Ludwig, happy to be free at last, and running to the

garden below, he pushed the long pump handle that brought the water rushing from the spout.

Up the long stairs he stumbled, the heavy pail dripping and splashing over the brim.

"You are a good boy, Ludwig, and a fine help to your mother," said Frau Beethoven, gently patting the dark tousled head.

Ludwig smiled happily and ran swiftly to his hiding place in the window seat near by, to curl himself up very small.

Now he could be alone by himself! If he pressed his face close against the windowpane, he could watch the children romping gaily in the garden below. Or he could look out over the housetops and away to the mountains beyond and dream strange dreams of far-away lands.

Wonderful melodies crept into his mind and sang to him gently as the hours rolled by and darkness fell softly over the hilltops.

Suddenly the sound of bells stole out upon the evening air. The carillon! Nothing in all the world did he love as much as the chiming bells. Whenever he was lonely or whenever he was sad, the ringing bells comforted him and made him happy again.

Now they were chiming more joyously than ever and like a flash, Ludwig ran down the back stairs and on to the palace. Standing beside the high tower, he listened breathlessly as the fine old bells played their glorious melodies for him.

When the last sweet chimes had died away, he sighed happily and crept back through the darkened streets to his home.

One morning, Mother Beethoven wakened the household earlier than usual.

"Come Ludwig, today we move to a new home, where your father can be nearer his work. You may help to carry the boxes to the Rhinegasse."

How glad Ludwig was to live on the riverfront, where he could watch the barges and boats go sailing by his very door.

And best of all was the old red ferry, the flying bridge, swinging like a pendulum from shore to shore, busily carrying its passengers across the swiftly flowing waters.

But there was little time on the Rhinegasse, for it was time to move again, this time to a smaller house, just across from the palace, where Father Beethoven could be still nearer his work.

Ludwig was delighted, for now he was closer than ever to his beloved carillon. Just as the twilight stole over the city, he ran to the window to watch the beautiful bells, turning and swinging as they played their melodies for him.

The old neighbors from the Bonngasse soon found their way to the new home with their instruments, for they could never do without their concerts.

One evening, as Father Beethoven carefully tuned his violin, he looked up to find Ludwig watching longingly.

"You may play the easy parts with us tonight, my son, but mind there are no mistakes!"

To play with the men! Ludwig ran to find his instrument and was soon in his place, his dark eyes shining. The music began, and proudly he drew the short bow across the strings, watching the notes very carefully so that he would be sure to keep up with the men.

Herr Ries smiled at the serious little violinist at his side.

"Well done, my little man!" he applauded, as the small musician put down his bow.

When the concert was over and the stands were put away, the neighbors left for their homes and soon the Beethoven household was quiet for the night.

Suddenly the sound of bells rang through the house, waking Ludwig from a sound sleep.

Yes, it was the carillon, but why was it ringing at this hour of the night?

Springing from his bed, he ran to the window and there was the bell tower, with tongues of fire leaping from every side!

"Mother! Father! The bells are burning! My beautiful bells!"

Down to the street he ran to watch the fire that raged and roared through the long night hours, making the sky as bright as day.

Higher and higher leaped the flames, and just as the bells began to play in the early dawn, they fell to the ground with a mighty crash.

Ludwig watched with horror as the tears crept down his cheeks. His beautiful bells were gone! They would never play for him again.

Now that he was seven years old, Ludwig started to school where he learned to read and write Latin and do simple sums in arithmetic.

But the lessons were very long and he was glad when it was time to leave so that he could play marbles with the boys on his way home.

But more than anything else, he loved to fly his homemade kite from the top of the hill when the wind was high. He liked to feel it tug and pull at the string in his hand as it soared far above his head, almost to the clouds.

In the Beethoven home, times were very difficult these days for Father Beethoven earned very little money, and soon pieces of silver and furniture were taken away to be sold, so that there would be food to eat.

But there was never enough, and at night when he went to bed, Ludwig tried hard not to think about the empty feeling inside him.

Mother Beethoven was sad as she went about her household tasks, struggling from early morning until late at night, trying to keep Ludwig and his two smaller brothers neat and clean.

And now Ludwig spent even longer hours at his practicing. If only there was some way that he could help, so that Mother Beethoven would not have to work so hard.

One morning, after a long lesson at the piano, Father Beethoven turned to his son.

"At last you are ready, Ludwig. It is time for you to play for the people of Bonn."

To give his first concert! Ludwig's eyes grew bright with eagerness. Every evening from then on, he sat at the old worn piano to play his pieces for the good neighbors who came to hear him, so that he would be sure to play well at the palace.

At last the special day arrived and Ludwig put on his splendid costume of a fine green tailcoat with vest of flowered satin, knee breeches and shoes with polished buckles, and a pigtail of real hair. At his side hung a

shining golden dagger.

Mother Beethoven looked proudly at her son.

"Good-bye, my Ludwig. Do the best that you can and you will surely bring us honor this day."

Ludwig strode away to the palace with Father Beethoven and when the great hall was quiet, he bowed solemnly, and seating himself at the piano, began to play.

His strong fingers flew over the keys with such power that the people sat up in wonder. This young boy was gifted, indeed!

When the concert was over, the people clapped their hands and shouted, "Bravo! Bravo!" and would not leave the hall until Ludwig sat to play his pieces over again.

Father Beethoven was well pleased and Ludwig was happy as they walked home in the early twilight.

"Now you must have a new master, my son, for you have learned all that I can teach you. Perhaps Herr Pfeiffer will work with you now."

Herr Pfeiffer! He was a very fine musician, but a stern taskmaster, indeed, and as soon as Ludwig began to work with the new teacher who had just come to the Beethovens to live, there were lessons at any time of the day or night.

Often, long after Ludwig had been in bed and asleep, Herr Pfeiffer shook him awake, and leading him to the piano, kept him at his practicing until the morning light found its way into the low dark cottage.

Sometimes, when the lesson went well, Herr Pfeiffer took out his silver flute and played lovely melodies for his pupil. And when Ludwig turned to the piano to make up an accompaniment, his teacher was pleased, indeed.

In the street outside, the people gathered around the open doorway to listen to the beautiful concert. On went the variations until at last Herr Pfeiffer put down his flute.

"Now Ludwig, you must sit here at the table and write this music that we have played together."

"But that I cannot do, Herr Pfeiffer, for I do not know the rules for writing music."

"Then there is no better time to learn. Come, I will teach you at once."

The lesson began, and after he had carefully explained some of the simple rules, Herr Pfeiffer started to leave for the theater.

"See to it that the music is finished when I return, young man!"

Poor Ludwig! The day had been long and hard and he was very weary. He bent over the paper and tried to write, but the notes would not come.

It was no use. Putting down his pen, he stumbled off to bed.

The hours rolled by and on he slept. Suddenly, in the middle of the night, someone shook him awake, calling loudly in his ear:

"Come, you lazy rascal! Up with you and finish the work that I left for you to do!"

Half asleep, Ludwig sat again at the table, Herr Pfeiffer close beside him, and slowly the notes went down on the paper.

Through the long night hours he struggled, many times falling sound asleep, his head resting heavily on his arms.

But always the thundering voice of his stern taskmaster brought him quickly back to his work.

Slowly the darkness began to fade and Herr Pfeiffer went off to bed, leaving his weary pupil to finish the last bit of writing.

The warm red glow of the rising sun crept in at the window as Ludwig turned to play what he had written.

Suddenly he paused and a smile lighted his face. He would play the music in his own way, instead — just as it sang itself in his mind!

Putting his hands on the keys, strong, ringing chords came from the instrument and sounded to every corner of the house. On and on went the music, rising and falling in singing melody.

Father Beethoven, awakened by the sounds, hurried to his friend.

"Pfeiffer! Pfeiffer! Only listen! It is our Ludwig who plays!"

"Yes, Johann — we have taught him well. It is good we started him early."

Mother Beethoven, busy with her cooking in the kitchen below, stopped her work to listen. Tears of joy filled her tired eyes.

"All is well," she whispered softly, "the boy has music in his heart!"

Father Beethoven hurried down to the kitchen.

"Wife — there will be no more school for our Ludwig. From this day on, he shall spend all of his time in music."

"But he is so young, Johann — only eleven."

"It is no matter. The boy will become a great musician, Maria," and he hurried away to speak to his son.

"Ludwig, it is time for you to play for the people of another country. Our friends are returning to their homes in Holland, and you and your mother will go with them. You will give a concert for the Dutch people, and perhaps make a name for yourself, like the boy Mozart!"

To go away to Holland! It seemed like a dream. Ludwig turned eagerly to his father.

"And when do we start?"

"In three days, when the boat will sail from the pier. There will just be time to make ready for the journey."

CHAPTER TWO

Ludwig hurried on board the riverboat with Mother Beethoven, his violin case under his arm. And just in time, for almost at once the whistle blew and away they sailed from the busy pier.

Father Beethoven stood on the dock below, calling above the noisy din as the boat headed out into the river.

"Good-bye! Good-bye! Bring us good luck, my son!"

The November day was clear and cold and Ludwig looked eagerly around him. He was off on a great adventure — to play for the people of Holland!

On down the Rhine they sailed, past mile after mile of gently winding hills, the rocky cliffs high above them crowned with old crumbling castles buried deep in the soft green pines.

As the sunlight faded into darkness, a sharp wind sprang up and it became bitterly cold. Mother Beethoven took the warm shawl from her shoulders and wrapped it snugly around her son, for a damp chill had settled over the water.

She was glad, indeed, when they landed in Rotterdam.

Ludwig liked the friendly Dutch people in their strange costumes, and rode through the low flat countryside to see the dykes and canals and swiftly whirling windmills, wheeling and shifting in the wind.

How good it was to be in the very country where Grandfather Beethoven had been born!

Before long, Ludwig was playing at the homes of royal families, dressed in his fine court costume. The

people were astounded at the skill of the young boy, and begged him to stay longer in their country and give them more concerts.

"Please come to live with us, and then we can have fine music all the year round," they urged.

But Ludwig had played all of his pieces, so it was time to return to Bonn, and away they sailed on the old river Rhine.

As they entered the small dwelling, Father Beethoven and the younger brothers called to them eagerly:

"Welcome home! Welcome home!"

Ludwig began to tell of his adventures, when suddenly the chiming of bells sounded through the quiet rooms. It was time for the service in the church!

There was no time to lose, for he could not miss the organ music. Speeding swiftly along the street, Ludwig came to a stone building, and creeping quietly through the doors of the church, he made his way to the front seat where he could watch Brother Willibald play the organ for the morning service.

As the music stole softly through the low chapel, Ludwig listened with all his might and wished more than ever that he could learn to play on the organ some day.

When the service was over and the people had left the church, Brother Willibald turned to leave the organ loft. Looking up, he saw a young boy sitting there alone.

"Good morning, my friend. Is there someone you wish to see?"

"No sir, I was just listening to the music," answered Ludwig in a small voice.

"Then perhaps you would like to see the organ," smiled the kindly Brother Willibald.

In a moment Ludwig was seated at the bench, and as his fingers ran swiftly over the keys, he listened breathlessly to the music that rang out through the tall pipes overhead.

"Ah, my young man, I see that you play the piano. But the organ has pedals, so the feet must work, as well as the hands, to make the rich bass notes sound."

He watched closely as Ludwig stepped on the long boards at his feet. It would not take long to teach this boy to play well.

"My friend, perhaps you and I can make a bargain. I could teach you to play on the organ and some day you would be able to help me with the services."

"Oh sir, I would be glad to learn," cried Ludwig earnestly. "And I will help you, too, if ever I can play well enough!"

The lessons began the very next day, and in a few short months, the young pupil had learned all that Brother Willibald had to teach him.

"You are ready to help me, now, Ludwig — and much sooner than I thought. At midweek you will take my place at the organ."

To play for the service in the chapel! Every day Ludwig spent most of his time at the organ, going over and over the music until he could play it all without once looking at the notes.

The special morning arrived and long before it was light, Ludwig started out through the frosty streets to the church. His fingers were numb with the cold and he blew on them and rubbed them hard to make them warm.

As the people came into the chapel, he put his hands on the keys and began to play. The music swelled through the small church and everyone looked up in astonishment to see a young boy sitting in the choir loft, playing the organ as they had never heard it played before!

Ludwig was never so happy, and from then on he helped Brother Willibald more and more, until he was playing every morning for the six o'clock service.

At the church of the Minorites not far away, was an even larger organ, and after making friends with the organist there, Ludwig helped him, too, playing for the special services each week, in return for lessons on the instrument.

On to the Münsterkirche went the eager young musician to make a bargain with Organist Zenser, the finest master of all.

Soon he was studying hard with his new teacher, who was delighted with the rapid progress of his eleven-year-old pupil, often inviting him to play for his older students.

One morning, after a lesson on the instrument, Ludwig quietly handed his teacher a roll of music that he had just finished.

"So, my young pupil — then you are a composer, as well as an organist!" smiled the master, looking at the closely written sheets. "But Ludwig — this is very difficult music — much too difficult for your small hands to play!"

"Oh, that does not matter, Herr Zenser," answered the young musician, quickly, "I will play it when I am bigger."

Ludwig loved the lessons at the organ and spent long hours in the church, practicing by himself. What fun it was to make up melodies as he went along, and then to see in how many ways he could make them sound!

Many times he hurried home to write the new music, and sometimes, when she was not too busy, Mother Beethoven sat to listen to the new compositions that her son played for her on the old piano.

"It is beautiful, Ludwig! Your father, too, will be well pleased with what you have done."

The best time of all the year was Mother Beethoven's birthday, when there was a fine celebration to honor her. As soon as darkness fell, and her chores were all finished for the day, she was hurried off to bed.

"Quickly, Karl and Johann — bring flowers and leaves!" called Ludwig to his younger brothers. "We must work fast, while Mother is asleep!"

Together they twined laurel and blossoms around the high-backed chair until it was a lovely bower for their queen.

Father Beethoven put the room in order, and when the table was piled high with good things and the stands were all in place, the neighbors crept in quietly with their instruments.

At last all was ready and Ludwig rapped softly on his Mother's door.

"Joyous birthday! Joyous birthday!" shouted the company, and as the stirring march began, Ludwig led Mother Beethoven, in her best Sunday costume, to her place on the throne, where she listened delightedly to the fine birthday concert.

Soon the little house was filled with merrymakers from far and near, and when the orchestra struck up its jolly tunes, the dancing began.

Ludwig played his violin with all his might as he watched his pretty mother. How good it was to see her smiling and happy!

Round and round went the merry company in their stockinged feet until far into the night. Ludwig was sorry when the first pale light of early morning crept in, for now it would be a whole year before there could be another birthday celebration.

Now that Herr Ries had been teaching him the violin,

Ludwig was joyous when he could play the more difficult parts of the music in the evening concerts.

He learned rapidly, indeed, and it was not long before he walked proudly to the palace with Father Beethoven, his violin under his arm. Now he was ready to take his place with the men in the orchestra, playing concerts for the Elector and his royal guests.

Sometimes the Elector played on his viola for the people, for he was very fond of music and wanted everyone in Bonn to like it, too.

He sent for the fine musician, Herr Neefe, to be the court organist, and Ludwig begged to go to the chapel to hear him whenever he played. If only he could study with the master some day, how much he would learn!

Whenever there was a minute to spare, Ludwig was busy composing pieces, sometimes for the piano and sometimes for the instruments of the orchestra, and Herr Ries was delighted whenever his pupil brought the new music to play for him.

"Ludwig, why not show your compositions to Herr Neefe? He is a composer himself, and perhaps he would help you with your writing."

For days Ludwig thought about the master, and at

last he decided to go to see him. Making his way to the chapel, he crept quietly to a corner of the room where the brilliant musician was seated at the organ, his fingers flying over the keys.

When the playing was finished, Ludwig quickly arose. He must go away at once, for surely this great master would not care to see his simple music!

The door creaked and Herr Neefe turned suddenly.

"Young man, did you wish to see me?"

It was no use — he could not leave now, and slowly Ludwig made his way to the organ.

"I — I am Ludwig Beethoven, sir, and I have brought some music that Herr Ries thought you might like to see."

Herr Neefe looked closely at the short, dark-haired boy.

"Writing melodies is all very well, young man. But first let me see what you can do in music."

The master gave him one difficult task after another, playing on the piano and the organ, and then on the violin and the viola.

Herr Neefe sat close by, nodding his head and beating time on the arm of his chair until Ludwig had finished.

"So! And you want to spend your life with music, young man?"

Looking seriously into the kind face above him, Ludwig answered quietly.

"I must become a musician, sir — there is nothing else for me to do."

Herr Neefe smiled.

"Yes! Yes! But there is much for you to learn, my boy. But if you are willing to work hard, come to me tomorrow and I will give you something to do."

Ludwig's dark eyes shone.

"Oh, thank you, Master Neefe, thank you, sir!" he cried breathlessly, and rushing home, he told good Mother Beethoven of the good fortune that had come to him.

In the long winter months, Ludwig worked harder with his new master than he had ever worked before. There were difficult works of Bach to be mastered, and lessons in composition, when he learned to write his melodies.

"Here, my young pupil, is a little march tune. Write the melody in nine different ways, and when you have finished the variations, bring them to me."

This was a task, indeed! Hurrying home, Ludwig began to work at once. On and on he wrote, and when at last the music was finished, he proudly took the closely written sheets to Herr Neefe.

But the master shook his head.

"No, Ludwig, it will not do. You have not followed the rules."

"But see, Herr Neefe, I will play it for you as I like it to sound!" cried Ludwig eagerly, going to the piano.

"Later, my young pupil," said the master severely. "But now the rules come first. Go home, young man, and write the music over again."

Sadly Ludwig began the long task, and when the writing was again finished, Herr Neefe was pleased.

"Yes, it is well done. Now we will send the music away to be printed."

To have copies made so that everyone might play his music!

Ludwig could hardly wait to see his first composition. At last it came, and proudly he read the words on the cover before him:

NINE VARIATIONS ON A MARCH
by Ludwig van Beethoven

Herr Neefe was glad to see his pupil so happy, and nodding his fine old head, he said to himself:

"Yes, and if this boy continues as he has begun, he will be another Mozart some day."

From then on, Herr Neefe helped his thirteen-year-old pupil in every way that he could, teaching him well, until he played with such power and skill that he was an even better pianist and organist than he, himself.

And now Ludwig was happy, indeed, for at last he was able to help the master who had been so kind to him, taking his place at the organ to play for the simple services whenever Herr Neefe was away from Bonn.

But even more than playing on the organ, Ludwig liked to compose pieces. Already in his book were compositions for the piano, some quartets for stringed instruments, and a long fugue for the organ.

He especially liked this little sonatina that perhaps you can play, too.

SONATINA
(TRACK 1)

Moderato

There were never enough hours in the day for his work, so Ludwig had to use the night, as well. But this was the best time of all, for now his mischievous brothers were asleep, and all was quiet in the small rooms, save for the river sounds, just outside.

It was good to hear the boats calling in deep tones as they sailed by through the night. And some- times they sounded close, as now, for the spring rains had made the river rise until it flooded all the countryside.

Ludwig went on with his work, and when the two compositions were finished, he went to the piano to try his jolly country dances, that you, too, will want to play.

ECOSSAISE - I
(TRACK 2)

ECOSSAISE - II
(TRACK 3)

As the sounds of the rollicking melodies danced through the night, the neighbors were awakened from sleep.

"It is only Ludwig playing again," they said drowsily.

When the music was just right, Ludwig carefully put the sheets in an old book and crept wearily to bed. He had not been asleep for long when his mother's voice rang in his ears.

"Ludwig! Ludwig! The river is rising! We must leave the house at once, or we are lost!"

In a moment he was beside Mother Beethoven, helping to rouse Father Beethoven and the sleeping children. Quickly they rushed to the stairs, but already the water had risen to their feet.

"The window — quickly!" shouted Ludwig, and into the night they called for help, but the roaring waters drowned their cries.

At last, when they had almost given up hope, a voice came faintly from the darkness.

"Beethoven! Beethoven! Johann! Ludwig!"

"Herr Ries! We are here!" called Ludwig, and soon they were climbing into the boat held fast for them by their good neighbor.

Through the long black night they rode on the swirling river and Ludwig listened to the Rhine as it went madly on its way, uprooting trees and houses and carrying them swiftly down the stream.

When the morning dawned, the river went down and in a few days the Beethovens were settled again. Ludwig hurried to his friend, Herr Neefe, to tell him of his exciting adventures.

"But my book of pieces is gone, Master Neefe — the river swept it away," said Ludwig sadly. "And there was such a nice little romance — it went like this," and going to the piano, he played his delightful composition that you will want to try, too.

ROMANCE
(TRACK 4)

"And now there is a new adventure waiting for you, my boy," smiled Herr Neefe, when Ludwig had finished playing. "A conductor is needed for the Elector's orchestra in the theater."

Ludwig could not wait for him to finish.

"And you think that I might try it, sir?" he asked breathlessly.

"Yes, Ludwig. Tomorrow the men will be waiting for their new leader. Good luck to you, my boy."

The next afternoon Ludwig made his way to the theater, and finding the musicians in their places with their instruments tuned, he sat at the piano, ready to conduct the orchestra.

The men were highly amused when they saw the young boy waiting to lead them. Someone was playing a trick on them!

"What is this? A child to direct us? But he will not go far. Young Master Beethoven will soon give up his difficult task," they said to one another.

Quietly Ludwig opened the book before him, and nodding to the musicians, the rehearsal began. But soon the music became too difficult and at once Ludwig stopped the men to play the parts over and over until they were able to go on again.

Why — this young boy was a fine musician, indeed! When the rehearsal was over, the members of the orchestra applauded him again and again.

"Bravo, Beethoven! Bravo, Conductor!" they cried lustily.

Ludwig was happy, indeed, as he hurried home through the quiet market square. The sun was setting as he pushed open the low door of the Beethoven home, and finding a letter waiting for him, he eagerly tore it open.

"At last, Father!" he cried joyously. "At last I bring you good luck! The Elector wishes me to assist Herr Neefe at the organ, with payment each year for my services."

Father Beethoven nodded gravely, while Mother Beethoven exclaimed proudly: "And well you deserve this honor that comes to you, my boy."

The sum of money was small, but it seemed very

large to Ludwig. And best of all, now Mother Beethoven would not have to work so hard.

After a scanty supper, Ludwig sped back to the chapel, where the royal choir was waiting to practice the church music. The fine young singer, Herr Heller, stood near by, impatient to begin his solo.

As Ludwig took his place at the organ, a twinkle came into his eye.

"Herr Heller, would you allow me to try to throw you off the solo part?"

The proud singer in rich costume smiled in amusement.

"My dear young Beethoven, that is something that no one could do. But you have my permission to try."

The music began and as the beautiful solo swept through the chapel, Ludwig played strange melodies, making the accompaniment more and more difficult, until Herr Heller could no longer keep his place.

"Stop, Beethoven, stop!" he shouted angrily. "I am lost with such bad playing."

Ludwig turned laughingly to the singer, when suddenly he spied the Elector seated at the back of the chapel!

Springing to his feet, he bowed low.

"I am sorry, your Majesty!" he murmured. "I did not know that you had honored us with your presence!"

The ruler was much amused, but he shook his finger at the young mischief-maker.

"You had better try a simpler accompaniment next time, young man. And remember — no more tricks in the future."

CHAPTER THREE

CHAPTER THREE

Easter morning dawned clear and still in sleepy little Bonn, lying quietly beside the swiftly flowing river.

But just as the sun climbed over the mountains to light the narrow cobbled streets, the bells from the palace and the high church towers wakened the good folk with their chiming and ringing as they joyously welcomed the festival day.

As the first sound stole through his small dark room, Ludwig sprang from his bed. It was Easter morning!

And soon it would be time for him to go to the palace, for Herr Neefe had gone away from the city, leaving him alone to play the difficult Easter music.

His first special service in the chapel! And the ruler of Bonn, with noblemen from far over the countryside would be there to hear him!

"Come, Ludwig — the porridge is ready," called Mother Beethoven from the kitchen below.

Quickly putting on his one good uniform, Ludwig hurried down to his simple meal and started on his way to the palace.

Through the old market square he went, where peasants in brightly colored costumes had been gathering together, winding their way down the steep mountain passes from their homes in the hills since long before daybreak, to be ready for the Easter celebration.

The music of the bells filled all the air, and Ludwig listened eagerly to their glad pealing as he went on his way. The bells! How he loved the chiming bells!

At the palace, royal guards in bright crimson uniforms stood at attention as noble families in costly silks and velvets, drove up in their fine carriages to pay their respects to the Elector.

Suddenly the guns on the old city walls fired a rousing salute, and when the last echoes had died away, the people silently made their way to the churches for the special Easter services.

It was time for him to play! Trembling with excitement, Ludwig took his place at the organ, his costume neat and his wig well in place.

As noble lords and ladies rustled by in rich silks and satins, he put his hands on the keys and the triumphant music began.

The beautiful melodies rang out through the shadowy chapel and the people listened in awe to the glorious Easter music that swept over them.

This young man was a fine organist, indeed! Yes — even better than their own Master Neefe.

"He is truly a wonder musician!" "His playing casts a magic spell!" "They say his name is Beethoven," they whispered to one another.

When the long service was over at last, Ludwig turned to leave the chapel and there, watching him proudly, stood Herr Neefe.

Ludwig started in surprise.

"Master Neefe! I did not know that you were here!"

"I returned to the city too late to play for the services, my boy. And it is better so, for I have heard your music. It was very beautiful, indeed."

He looked long at the broad-shouldered young man before him.

"Ludwig, it is time now for you to have a new master. You must go to Vienna and study with the great Mozart."

Wolfgang Mozart! The noted master and composer! But Vienna was a long way off and there was no money, so how could he go?

Quietly he went on with his work, dreaming night and day of the master in Vienna. Mozart! Mozart! Over and over the name sang itself in his mind. He must try to earn a little money, and perhaps some day there would be enough to take him to the far-off city.

Whenever there was special music to be played at the palace, there was payment for his services, and away went Ludwig to drop the precious coins in a small box, kept safely on a high shelf in the old cupboard.

One day, as he was slipping a penny under the lid, it fell from his fingers and rolled away. Quickly he tried to stop it, but on it went, down through a crack in the floor. And when every penny was needed so badly!

Suddenly a melody rushed into his mind — a melody about the penny. He must write it down at once! The notes went quickly onto the paper and soon his little "Anger Over a Lost Penny" was finished.

Can you hear the part where he is angry?

ANGER OVER A LOST PENNY
(TRACK 5)

As the years went slowly by, the little fund could not grow, for always something was needed in the Beethoven home, and Ludwig could not bear to see Mother Beethoven or his younger brothers without food or clothing.

The box was empty now, but one day, long after he had given up hope of ever going to Vienna, a knock sounded through the low rooms, and there in the doorway stood Herr Neefe, a letter in his hand.

"Your dream has come true, Ludwig! Word has just come from the Elector that he wishes to send you to Vienna, to study with the composer, Mozart!"

To go to Vienna at last! Ludwig could hardly believe the words that rang in his ears.

It did not take him long to get ready, and soon he was on his way, jogging over the bumpy roads in the rickety open coach.

The April rain fell steadily throughout the long afternoon, and before nightfall Ludwig was cold and wet to the skin. But he did not mind — he was on his way to the master, in Vienna!

At last, on a starry night in May, he arrived at the end of his journey.

Vienna! The home of Mozart! Ludwig was too excited to sleep, and early the next morning he hurried through the winding streets to the home of the composer.

The door opened, and there, at the end of the long room with his friends gathered around him, was the great master!

Mozart smiled a welcome to the strange young man in rough clothing, with his black, bushy hair standing on end.

"So — you are Ludwig Beethoven?"

"Yes, sir. I have come from Bonn to play for you, sir."

"Very well, young man. Now then, let me see what you can do," and leaning back in his chair, the master listened quietly as the music began.

Yes, this young Beethoven played very well, indeed, but in Vienna there were many young men who played well.

As the composer rose slowly from his chair, the music stopped suddenly and Ludwig sprang to face him, his dark eyes burning deeply.

"Oh sir, you must not go! Only give me a melody and I will show you at once what I can do in music!"

The master looked into the eager young face, lighted with a strange fire, and going to the piano, he played a melody with a hard catch in it. This would be a test for the boy from Bonn!

Ludwig sat breathlessly at the piano and for a moment he was lost in deep thought. Then, putting his hands on the keys, he began to play and the room was filled with glowing music, now joyous, now slow and stately, and ending with strong ringing chords — all woven from the little melody.

A pleased smile stole over the face of the master. Here was a musician, indeed! Quietly he spoke to his companions. "Keep your eyes on this young man. He will make a noise in the world some day."

Mozart liked his music! Ludwig wanted to shout for joy, for now there would be lessons with the master!

Soon he was at work with the great teacher, listening with all his might as the composer taught him more about the writing of his music.

This andantino of his has such a delightful melody. And you will enjoy playing the variation, as well.

ANDANTINO
(TRACK 6)

Variation

But the lessons soon came to an end, for on a warm day in July, Ludwig was called home to Bonn. He was very sad, indeed, for Mother Beethoven had died.

Now he must earn a living for Father Beethoven and the two younger brothers, and soon he was at work, playing the organ in the chapel and the violin in the theater, and giving lessons to pupils.

But no matter how hard he struggled, from early morning until late into the night, there was still not enough money to keep the little family together.

Soon he became very ill, indeed, for there had not been food enough to eat, or time for rest.

His good pupil, Stephen Breuning, came quickly to help, and at once took him to his beautiful home, where kind Frau Breuning tenderly cared for the young musician until he was strong and well again.

In the evenings, the children crowded around him, begging him for music.

"Play for us, Ludwig! Play for us!" they cried, and soon his melodies wove a magic spell over the beautiful home.

This little rondo of his they especially liked. Perhaps you can play it, too.

RONDO
(TRACK 7)

How good it was to be with his kind friends, with merry picnics along the banks of the river on bright sunny days, or mountain climbing when the air was crisp and clear and the forests were dressed in scarlet and gold.

Many times Count Waldstein, the young musician and friend of the Elector, went with them, and soon he and Ludwig became good friends.

He was very kind, indeed, sending Ludwig a fine new piano and many pupils to teach, and often arranged concerts for him to play at the homes of his noble friends.

One morning, as Ludwig sat at the shiny new piano, the young count burst merrily into the room.

"An invitation I bring you, Ludwig! Herr Haydn will stop to visit us on his way home from England, and he wishes to entertain the musicians of Bonn at a breakfast."

"Waldstein! The noted composer, Joseph Haydn!" exclaimed Ludwig excitedly. "No greater honor could you bring me, my friend!"

Suddenly an idea came to him. He would write a new composition and show it to the great master when he arrived in the city.

The special morning dawned, and in the bright sunshine the two friends hurried to the beautiful gardens, where the great Haydn waited to greet them.

After a fine breakfast under the stately old trees, Ludwig went quietly to the master to lay the new music on the table before him.

Haydn looked carefully at the closely written pages, and looking up, he smiled warmly at the young composer.

"Your cantata is very good, young Beethoven, very good, indeed. I would be glad to give you help with your music, if you could arrange to come to me in Vienna."

"Oh thank you, Master Haydn!" exclaimed Ludwig breathlessly. "Perhaps some day I will be able to accept your kind offer."

Early the next morning, Count Waldstein mounted his favorite horse, and galloping to the door of his friend, called out his good news.

"Luck is with you today, Ludwig! The Elector has heard of Haydn's wish to help you with your music, and he wishes to send you to gay Vienna, to work there with the noted master."

To go back to the city of music!

"Bravo! Bravo! Bravo!" shouted the friends together, as they danced gaily around the room.

Before dawn the next morning, the post clattered briskly over the cobblestones and Ludwig stepped inside. Beside the rushing river he jolted along and was soon on the highway leading to Vienna.

When at last he arrived in the city, he found himself a small attic room in the house of the noble Prince Lichnowsky and was soon learning how to write his melodies with master Haydn in his little house, just outside Vienna.

This delightful Minuetto of his you will surely enjoy.

MINUETTO
(TRACK 8)

The young pianists of Vienna welcomed Ludwig among them, for they had heard of his fine playing and were eager to hear him. At once a contest was arranged to see who could improvise the best.

"Come, Beethoven, it is your turn now," called the young men, when each had finished playing.

Quietly Ludwig took his place at the piano, and with the brilliant musicians leaning breathlessly over the instrument, the little melody grew beneath his fingers, one difficult variation after another, until the young pianists broke into excited applause, crying out in wonder:

"A miracle man! Bravo! Bravo! Beethoven is the winner!"

Shabby clothes would never do now, and there must be dancing lessons as well, so from his precious store of ducats, Ludwig took just enough to buy black silk stockings. And now with his new flowered cravat, made especially for him by kind Frau Breuning, he looked like a young nobleman, indeed.

Often Prince Lichnowsky invited him to come down to the palace rooms to play for his royal guests.

One evening, after the beautiful compositions were

ended, the prince spoke to the young pianist.

"Beethoven, you have given me great pleasure with your music, and now I would be happy if you would come to live with me, here in the palace, and conduct my orchestra."

Ludwig could hardly believe the words of the nobleman. To live in the palace and lead one of the finest orchestras in all Vienna!

Quietly he gave his answer to the prince.

"Thank you, Your Highness. I would be glad to accept your kind offer."

The next day all was settled, and putting his few possessions under his arm, Ludwig left his attic room and made his way downstairs to the richly furnished quarters, where special servants were waiting to attend him.

He felt like a king, indeed, but soon he was at work again, conducting the orchestra, composing, and giving lessons to pupils of noble families.

In the evening, when there were no concerts at the palace, he liked to walk with his friend Cramer in the beautiful gardens in Vienna and listen to the music played by the orchestra.

As the joyous melodies of Mozart came through the dimly lighted trees, Ludwig swayed and danced to them, his arms floating through the air.

"Oh Cramer, Cramer!" he cried, "you and I will never make melodies like the master, Mozart!"

Steadily his own compositions grew, one lovely piece after another.

This merry rondo you will want to play again and again.

RONDO
(TRACK 9)

When the warm summer days came to the city, Ludwig went with Master Haydn to the country, and when he returned again to the palace, he found waiting for him a fine gift from the prince — a beautiful black riding horse, with a groom to care for him.

But alas for the poor horse and groom! Day after day they waited patiently at the door for their new master. But Ludwig had forgotten all about them, for he was hard at work on a new composition, and as soon as it was finished, he hurried away with it to his new masters, Albrechtsberger and Salieri.

"So!" exclaimed Salieri sternly, after he had carefully

examined the music before him. "And still you do not follow the rules that I have taught you!"

"But sir," explained Ludwig seriously. "That I cannot do, for I must write as I feel. That is the way the music sings itself in my mind."

Anxiously the two masters talked together.

"It is no use. We can teach him nothing, for he will never learn according to rule."

But Ludwig was feeling something that no one could teach him, and he went on his way alone, writing as no one had ever written before, putting into his music the great thoughts that burned in his mind, music breathing happiness and love for all mankind.

As the years went by, many friends of the prince found their way to the palace to see his brilliant young conductor, and soon all of Ludwig's time was spent in playing for them.

Anxiously he spoke to the friend who came to visit him.

"Wegeler, I must leave the palace now, for there is no longer time for my composing. And every day there is dinner at four, so I must be home in time to put on better clothes and care for my beard. I cannot stand it longer! Help me, Wegeler — I must go away at once!"

Quickly packing his belongings, he said good-bye to the prince, and moving to a simple little room, he was happy again, for now no one could disturb him at his composing, and he could go about as he pleased in his old worn clothing.

Many times he went back to visit the good nobleman, and when his first concerto was finished, he went with it to the palace, and giving the men of the orchestra their parts, he sat at the piano, and together they played the brilliant composition for his kind friend.

"Bravo, Ludwig! The music is beautiful!" exclaimed the prince heartily. "Now you must play it for the people of Vienna."

The practicing began at once, and when there were no mistakes, the concerto was played in the old Burg Theater and the applause of the audience rang throughout the hall.

To think that the people liked his music! Ludwig was so happy that he decided to travel to other large cities and give concerts.

Off he started, and arriving in Berlin, he delighted the audiences there with his fine playing.

On to Leipzig he journeyed, where the king received him graciously, inviting him to play at his royal court, and presenting him with a beautiful ring when the concert was over.

But Ludwig was glad to return to Vienna, where his good friends eagerly awaited him.

"Welcome, Ludwig! Welcome home!" they cried, leading him through the streets to his room.

A fine hot supper was waiting, with instruments made of pastry as a surprise, and around the room went the jolly merrymakers, singing at the tops of their voices as they played on their toy instruments, gobbling them up when the procession was ended.

Already Ludwig had written quartets, trios, sonatas, and a song. And now that his first symphony was finished, it was time to give another concert for the people of Vienna, this time all of his own works!

The prince was delighted at the good news and at once sent invitations far and near, inviting everyone to the greatest concert of all the year, to be given by the composer, Ludwig van Beethoven.

Every morning at eight o'clock, Ludwig and the men were in their places at the palace, and the practicing began.

GRAND MUSICAL CONCERT
BY
MR. L. VAN BEETHOVEN
which will take place
Tomorrow March 28, 1801
in the Burg Theatre
The musical pieces to be performed are the latest works of Mr. Ludwig van Beethoven

The good prince listened, patiently, and as hour after hour rolled by and the music went on, he sent for baskets of bread and rich juicy sausages for the hungry, weary men.

At last all was ready, and when the special night arrived, the theater was crowded to the doors with the eager audience, with the proud Prince Lichnowsky and his royal company seated close to the stage.

When all was quiet, Ludwig came to the platform amid a storm of applause, and bowing low, he seated himself at the piano near the orchestra.

The music began and there was not a disturbing sound in the long hall. The young composer looked like a king, indeed, sitting so straight and calm in his fine new uniform, his brilliant melodies flowing from his fingers in such rich, singing tone, that the audience could be still no longer, and broke into excited applause.

But Ludwig did not like to be interrupted, for he could never play when there was noise, so he waited patiently until the hall was quiet before going on again with the concert, now to conduct the orchestra in his first symphony, so filled with joyous melody.

The audience was astounded at the power of the brilliant young composer. How proud they were that he lived with them in their own city of Vienna!

"A wonder composer! Bravo! Beethoven! Beethoven!" echoed their cries to every corner of the theater.

And now, throughout the city of Vienna and in all the cities near by, the name of Beethoven was spoken everywhere, and eager visitors made their way to his door, begging to study with him, and calling for more concerts.

But Ludwig could not hear them, for a sickness had settled in his poor ears, making them buzz and ring all day long.

Even at night he could get no rest, and when the noise grew to a loud roaring sound that would not stop, he sent for the great Doctor Schmidt to come to visit him.

When the long examination was over, Ludwig anxiously looked into the solemn face above him.

"But my ears, Herr Schmidt — surely they will be well soon?"

Quietly the doctor laid his hand on Ludwig's shoulder.

"For a little time they may be better, but the sickness will come again," he answered gravely.

As the hours passed slowly by and darkness settled over the room, Ludwig sat alone in his chair.

Putting out his hand, he touched the piano that he loved so well. Never to hear its music again? And never to hear the glad voices of his friends?

Then he must go away at once, for never must they know that he could not hear them when they called his name.

Quickly packing a few belongings, he climbed into the lumbering coach in the drizzling rain, and with eyes closed and head bowed low, he rode slowly away from the city of music.

CHAPTER FOUR

The warm summer sun smiled gently
on the beautiful little village of
Heiligenstadt, lying just outside the busy city of Vienna.

There, half asleep in the long grasses, a tumbledown
miller's cottage stood beside a trickling stream, the old
windmill overhead swinging its ragged arms in the lazy
breeze.

But the lonely Beethoven, sitting in the open doorway
in his worn, faded green coat, could not hear the whirring
sound above him as he dreamed away, looking out over
the wide rolling meadows to the mountains beyond, still
wearing their glistening caps of snow.

Suddenly the wind rushed down from the mountains
and across the broad fields, tossing the long grasses and
piling the thunder clouds in dark masses overhead.

A thunderstorm! Beethoven smiled as the heavy drops
of rain spattered to the ground, and turning quickly to

the little kitchen where a peasant boy was busy with household chores, he called lustily:

"Hans! Hans! My hat!"

"Yes, Master!"

Rushing about the cottage, the brown-skinned boy searched everywhere, but the hat could not be found.

Suddenly he burst into merry laughter, his brown eyes twinkling with mischief.

"Come! Come, Hans! This is no time for playing! Why do you not bring the hat?" demanded Beethoven sternly.

Quickly the boy wrote on the little pad hanging from the master's neck.

"The hat is on the head, sir!"

Beethoven smiled.

"So! So!" he chuckled, and patting Hans on the shoulder, he put his notebook under his coat and strode over the fields, lifting his face to the heavens and laughing joyously as the rain pounded down on him.

As the thunder crashed and roared through the valley, the ground trembled beneath his feet and strong music began to ring in his mind.

Quickly! He must write it down at once, or it might be lost forever.

Rushing to a pine tree, he crouched beneath its wide-spreading branches, and with his big carpenter's pencil, he wrote the notes as fast as his hand could travel.

Dusk had fallen, and with hat gone and his bushy head bowed, he found his way back to the cottage, hearing nothing but the melodies that were working in his mind, music that told of his struggle to conquer the deafness that was slowly shutting him away from the world.

(TRACK 10)

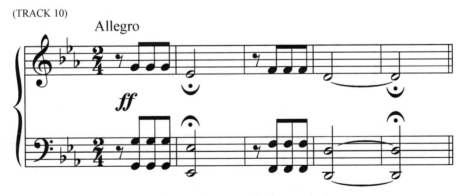

…thundered the mighty tones.

From the kitchen, Hans and Mother Anna brought steaming bowls of food and put them on the table near by.

"The supper is laid, sir."

But the master did not hear as he stamped around the room, pounding out the time of his great symphony on the table and upsetting the ink into the piano as he sat to play this lovely andante melody of the second part, so filled with comfort and hope.

(TRACK 11)

On through the night hours labored the master, bending low over the keys to the ear trumpet to catch what he could of the sounds of beauty.

At last the pattern of the glorious Fifth Symphony was laid out, ending with the stirring song of victory. If he could no longer play for people, he would give them something even better — his noble music to enjoy.

Through the long summer months, in every kind of weather, Beethoven roamed through the woods and fields.

And even at night, long after the sun had set behind the purple mountains, he could not go to bed, for he must walk in the restful moonlight and lie in the meadows to gaze up at the stars and the clouds, for in them he found peace.

The night wind stirred in the pines over his head and the birds called softly from their nests. But Beethoven could not hear them.

As he sadly watched his beloved nature world around him, he remembered the sounds, and wrote in his notebook the lovely melodies that came to him.

This beautiful minuet in G, you will want to play many, many times.

MINUET IN G

(TRACK 12)

Trio

D.C. al Fine

One morning, as Beethoven roamed joyously over the flowering hillsides, he came suddenly upon a village carnival, with peasants dancing merrily in their brightly colored costumes.

He must dance, too! In a moment, Beethoven joined in the merrymaking, laughing heartily as he whirled about.

"Ho-la! Ho-la! Ho-la-la!" he cried, stamping his feet in time to the measure.

Suddenly he left the jolly company and the peasants watched in amazement as the stranger danced away across the fields, wheeling and turning and waving his arms as he sang in a loud voice the rollicking music that filled his mind.

Running into the cottage, he played his new country dances so merrily that soon Hans and Anna were moving gaily around the kitchen to his music, ending their dance with loud clapping of hands and stamping of feet.

Can you play these jolly country dances of his?

COUNTRY DANCE
(TRACK 13)

COUNTRY DANCE

Beethoven could not forget the merry peasants at the carnival, whirling about in the bright sunlight. Perhaps they were still there! Off he started over the meadows, his loose green coat flying behind him in the breeze.

This was a joyous day, indeed, for his ears were a little better and now he could hear the wistful tune of the shepherd as he piped away on the hill.

Quickly he wrote it in his notebook:

(TRACK 15)

On through the fields went the master. Yes, there were the peasants, dancing gaily to the music of the country fiddler, sawing away on his old violin, playing his three notes over and over for the rollicking company.

Suddenly a flash of lightning and muttering thunder sent the merrymakers scurrying to the trees for shelter. Down came the shower, but soon it was gone, and the sun shone on the glowing rainbow, arching from heaven

to earth. All nature seemed to sing a song of thanks, now that the storm was over.

Why, this would make a good symphony! It could be a pastoral symphony — music of the nature world, with the

114

shepherd's song, the peasants gathering for the festival, a thunder shower, and ending with this beautiful hymn of thanksgiving. He must start it at once!

115

Allegretto

How the master loved the green countryside of Heiligenstadt! He must write to his friend, Wegeler, and tell him of his joy. Reaching for his pencil, he began.

Dear friend,

How glad I am to be here, able to roam in wood and thicket, among the trees and flowers and rocks! No one can love the country as I do. Woods, trees, and rocks give back the joy that my heart longs for. In the country every tree has a voice and seems to speak to me, saying, 'Holy! Holy!' My bad hearing does not trouble me here so much, for in the woods there is enchantment and peace — sweet peace of the woods!

Your Beethoven

But now the cold winds had begun to sweep down from the mountains and the early morning frosts chilled the little cottage, so it was time to go back to Vienna.

When he arrived in the old city, his good friends were there to welcome him home.

"Come Ludwig! Such fine rooms I have found for you!" exclaimed Wegeler. "You shall see them for yourself," and taking his friend by the arm, he led him to a simple dwelling near by.

Beethoven walked quietly to the windows and looked out onto the narrow street.

"But where are the trees?" he asked anxiously.

"Trees?" echoed the astonished landlord. "There are no trees."

"Then I cannot take the rooms," and turning away, Beethoven left the house.

At last a suitable place was found, and as soon as he was settled, Beethoven invited his friends to dinner. He would make them some soup — they would like that!

When the special night arrived, he hurried to the door to greet his guests, with a nightcap on his head, an apron tied around his waist, and a long ladle in his hand.

"Welcome to the home of Cook Beethoven!" he cried merrily.

Soon he was waiting on his guests, serving them the food that he had worked so hard to prepare — watery soup, burned vegetables, and dried-up meat.

Poor Beethoven! With his composing, there was little time to look after his household, and soon his rooms were in such disorder that he could find nothing in them.

And now a part of his great Mass in D, was lost! Perhaps it was in the kitchen. He hurried to see and there, wrapped around his old boots and the pots and pans, was the beautiful music, wrinkled and soiled and torn!

Perhaps if he moved to a new house, all would be better.

He set out at once, and when he found rooms that suited him, he carried off a part of his belongings, leaving the rest to come later.

When the springtime came, he had moved four times, and now all of his fine pianos were without legs, for with so many movings, there had not been time to put them on again.

But things grew steadily worse, and at last he called upon the wife of one of his good friends to help him.

"Dear Frau Streicher, so good you are to come! Too many troubles I have here. I must carry in my head so many pairs of trousers and socks, or they are lost in the wash. And could you tell me, please, how I could get good meals here at home? My servant can no longer see, taste, or smell, so that my poor stomach is always in danger."

One morning, not long afterward, the master returned from a long walk to find a messenger at his door.

"Sir, the King of Westphalia has sent me to deliver a message to the great composer, Beethoven."

"My name is Beethoven," answered the master quietly.

"Then, sir, the ruler of Westphalia wishes you to come to live at his court in Cassel, to be his Kappelmeister there."

To have no more household worries — how good that would be!

But no sooner did Prince Lichnowsky hear of the news than he hurried to the master's rooms with his noble friends.

"Beethoven, we have heard of the message of King Jerome, and we would like to offer you the post of Composer to the Court of Vienna, with a yearly sum in payment for compositions that you will write for our theater."

The master listened quietly until the nobleman had finished.

"Gentlemen, I thank you for your kind offer, which I will accept."

Joyfully the noblemen left the bare dwelling. Now Vienna would not lose her great composer!

At once came the order for new music to be written for the opening of the theater, and shutting himself up in his rooms, he began to compose the Turkish March for a play called "The Ruins of Athens."

How warm it was in the cramped quarters! Going to a basin in the corner, he filled the large jug with cold water, and pouring it over his head and hands, he put a wet towel around his neck and went back to his work.

Suddenly there was a loud knocking, and when the door opened, there stood the angry landlady who lived in the rooms just below.

"Herr Beethoven — you have ruined my house! Everywhere from the ceiling the water is pouring down!" she shouted, pointing to the pools on the floor at her feet.

"Then I shall have to move, Madame, for I must keep cool for my work."

Back to his table went the master and soon the stirring new composition was finished, with the martial tread of the Turkish soldiers resounding through the city streets.

How you will enjoy playing this duet with someone!

TURKISH MARCH
(TRACK 17)

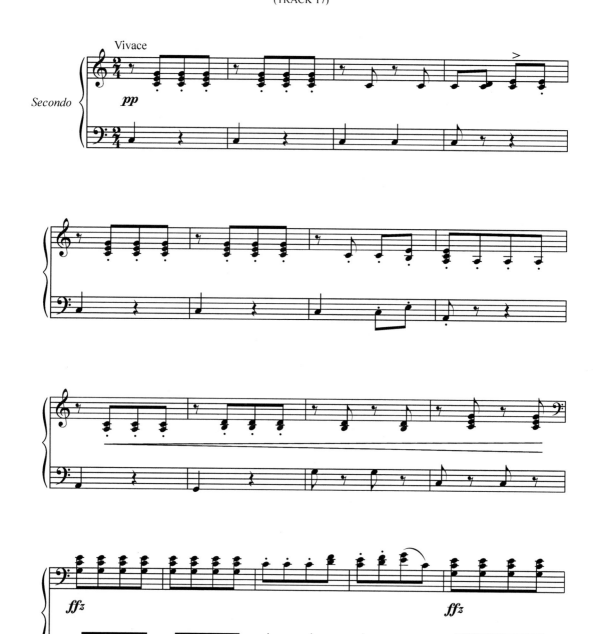

TURKISH MARCH
(TRACK 18)

(TRACK 19 is the TURKISH MARCH - Primo & Secondo Duet)

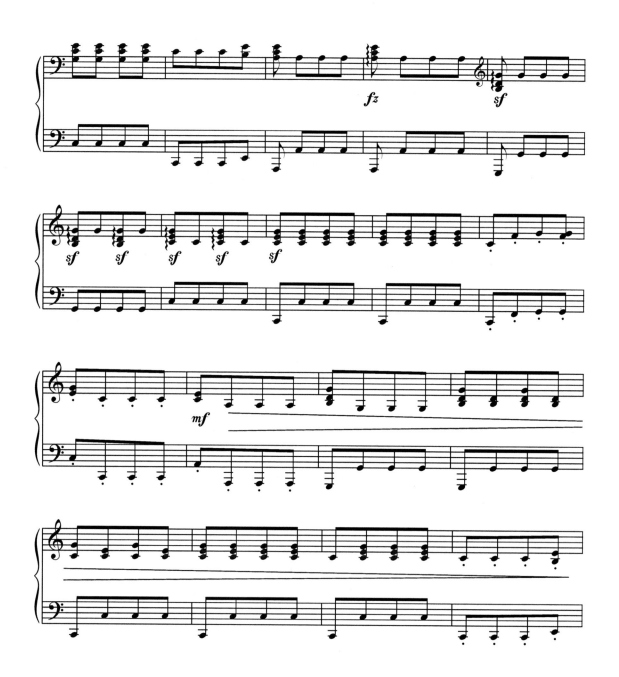

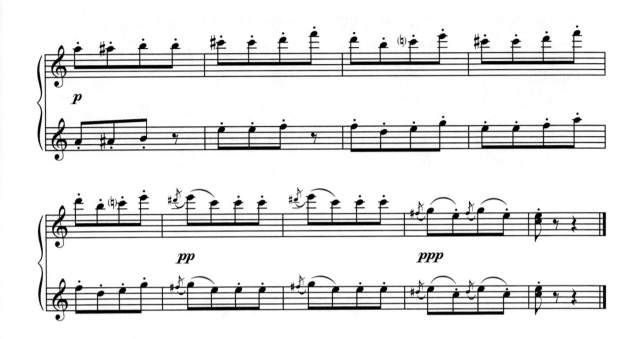

The gay city of Vienna was filled with bustle and excitement, for the great Congress was soon to meet, when the nobles throughout the land would gather together.

There must be very special entertainment for this rare occasion, and at once the officials of Vienna made their way to the door of the master, begging him to honor the city with a performance of his works.

Beethoven was delighted and set to work on his opera, Fidelio, for the special event.

At last the night of the great festival arrived and the large hall was crowded to the doors with royal visitors from far and near, listening in wonder to the music of the opera, Fidelio.

When the curtain went down, the bravos of the audience sounded again and again until the master came to the platform to bow to the excited people.

"Bravo! Beethoven! Beethoven! Beethoven!" greeted him on every side.

The Empress of Russia, royal princes from foreign lands, and lords and ladies of Vienna heaped costly presents and large sums of money on the famous composer, and the name of Beethoven rang throughout the countryside.

"Ah, my good Stephen," smiled the master as his friends gathered joyfully around him, "even my poor ears cannot make me too sad now. Come, you and I must celebrate this fine occasion! We will go away to Baden, and who knows — perhaps someone there may be able to help me."

In a few days Stephen Breuning and Beethoven were off to the well-known place of cures. Here, though he sought far and wide, there was no help for his poor ears and Beethoven was soon lost in his composing, working harder than ever on his Seventh and Eighth Symphonies, where he found peace and happiness.

As he wandered alone through the quiet countryside that he loved so well, a delightful composition came into his mind, and in the flowering meadow, he sat to write this lovely minuet. Hasn't it a beautiful melody?

MINUET

As he wandered on to the end of the fields, the sweet sound of bells broke the stillness of the valley, and there, lying before him in the peaceful sunlight, was a little monastery.

The heavy door stood open, and at the end of the low chapel was an organ.

How good it would be to play again! Going eagerly to the bench, Beethoven put his hands on the keys and the music stole softly through the church, growing richer and more powerful and ever more beautiful until the peasant women, busy with their sweeping, put down their brooms to listen.

Through the open doorway glided black-robed monks, and as the mighty music swept over them, they knelt in the aisles to pray.

One by one, the village folk left their work and crept in to listen, and soon the little chapel was filled with awestruck worshipers, listening in wonder to the music of the master.

When the long restful summer was over, Beethoven and Stephen said good-bye to lovely Baden and settling themselves in the carriage, set out for Vienna.

It was dusk when they arrived at the composer's door, and from the half darkness, a young boy ran swiftly to greet the master.

"Uncle Ludwig, I have come to live with you!" he announced in a high clear voice.

Beethoven smiled and put the ear trumpet close to the boy's lips.

"I am Karl, and you are my Uncle Ludwig, and I have come to live with you," he shouted.

A tall man stepped quickly to the boy's side.

"What Karl has told you is true, sir. His father has just died, leaving him in your care."

To have a son of his own! A warm smile stole over the face of the master as he looked eagerly into the face of the dark-eyed child.

"You are welcome, Karl!" he said gently, and putting his arm around the young boy's shoulder, he led him to his new home.

And now the hours in the day were not long enough to care for Karl, so there was nothing to do but give up his composing.

His boy must have the finest education, and carefully Beethoven put away for him the large sum of money that had come from the last concert.

In the long hard years that went slowly by, there were many anxious times, but the fund for Karl was never touched. There was very little money and away to the country they carried their few belongings and soon were settled in a poor little house by the roadside.

Many times there was no food in the dark cottage, and putting on his old, worn-out shoes, the master tramped the long miles into the city to sell his compositions, so that Karl would have food.

At last it was time to send his boy away to school, and Beethoven was left alone. Soon he found his way back to Vienna and quietly his friends gathered around him, bringing him food and clothing and answering his simple needs.

Every morning early, even before the sun was up, he arose to make his coffee, allowing just sixty beans to the cup. After long hours at his composing, he walked by the old city walls at sunset, finding his way to an inn for a lonely dinner at night.

Sadly he missed his Karl and was glad, indeed, to be near his friend Stephen, whose little son Gerhardt, loved to visit with the master in his small bare room.

"Trouser Button!" Beethoven would exclaim, as the sunny head peeped in at the door. "Come now, a fine poem for your old friend."

Long hours they spent together, the fair-haired boy reciting his poems for the master, who could hear no sound, but watched with delight the gentle visitor on his knee.

One evening, as he sat dreaming near his piano, the door opened softly, and there, standing before him, was his old friend, Count Waldstein.

"Welcome! Welcome, my good Count!" cried the master, warmly. "But we must not stay here, Waldstein, for the moon is giving us her blessing. Come, my friend, we will walk in her light."

As they wandered happily through the narrow streets of the city, sounds of music came from a small dwelling near by.

"Ludwig! Someone is playing one of your sonatas! Come, let us go in."

Bending their heads, they went quietly into the poor little home, and there, in the half darkness, a blind girl sat at an old worn-out harpsichord, searching among the keys for the notes that she wished to play.

Gently the master spoke to her.

"I heard your music in passing. I will play for you now, if you wish."

A joyous smile lighted the girl's face as Beethoven sat at the poor instrument and in the low, flickering candlelight, his music wove a magic spell over the little home.

Quietly the young brother at his cobbler's bench put

down his work to listen. Who was this strange man, filling their simple cottage with such music?

Suddenly the candle flickered and went out and as Waldstein quietly flung open the shutters, the moonlight flooded the room and the glorious music swept on.

Breathlessly the blind girl leaned forward, afraid to miss a single note.

"You — you are Beethoven!" she whispered.

Quietly the master pushed back his chair.

"Good night," he answered gently, and hurrying through the streets to his small room, he worked until daylight to set down the music of his beautiful Moonlight Sonata.

This allegretto from the sonata you will want to listen to many times.

ALLEGRETTO
(TRACK 21)

As the years went slowly by, the great lonely composer could no longer play for the people of Vienna, for he could not hear the smallest sounds. His suffering had made him as strong as an oak and his long, bushy hair had grown quite white.

One night, after he had finished his simple meal at the inn, he sat in a corner with his eyes closed, smoking his long pipe, while the last bits of his Ninth Symphony worked themselves out in his mind.

As he dreamed away, he felt a hand rest gently on his arm. Looking up, a happy smile stole over his face and a piercing light shone in his dark eyes as he saw the friend who had been so faithful all of these years.

"Stephen!" he exclaimed joyously, holding out the pad and pencil hanging from his neck.

"A message has come to you from the people of Vienna," wrote Stephen, putting into his hands a long scroll.

Opening the paper, Beethoven read aloud:

"The people of Vienna humbly beseech their world-famous composer, Ludwig van Beethoven, to grant them the honor of performing for them for the first time, his Ninth Symphony, and his great Mass, the Missa Solemnis."

The master started to his feet, tears of joy in his kindly dark eyes.

"Stephen! Stephen! To think that this honor has come to me! But I must go home at once, for the symphony is not yet finished!"

As he stumbled off through the darkened streets, he came to a little church. It was just time for the evensong! Yes, there were the old bells, turning and swinging over his head, pealing their gentle music at the close of day.

The tower bells! If he could only hear the chiming tower bells!

But the sounds rang only in his mind and sang to him gently that night as the notes of the Ninth Symphony poured from his pen in a flood of joy.

At last the music was ready, and when the night of the great concert arrived, Beethoven stood in his doorway, ready to leave.

The old housekeeper, Frau Schnapps, sadly shook her head as she helped him into his shabby, faded green coat.

"Oh, Master! Master! On such a night as this, and not one good coat to wear!"

But Beethoven was never so happy. He hurried away through the cobbled streets, smiling up at the stars that glowed softly over his head as he made his way to the theater where all of Vienna waited breathlessly for him.

As he walked to the platform with his old green coat flowing behind him, the audience stood to honor their beloved Beethoven, composer of the greatest symphonies that the world has ever known.

When the waves of applause had died away, the master raised his hand and the glorious Ninth Symphony, so filled with happiness, began. The song of joy rang exultingly throughout the long hall:

(TRACK 22) Allegro

When the concert was over, a storm of applause came from the audience, their cries resounding again and again.

"Long live Beethoven! Long live our great composer!"

But the master could not hear them, and as a singer turned him gently to face the audience, the noble head bowed low as he saw from the flutter of handkerchiefs, the applause that rained upon him.

A smile of heaven shone on his face and softly he whispered:

"I write not for you, but for those who shall come after."

And so the greatest master of all, born in a little cold attic room, and longing for joy and happiness, has given his glorious music to you and me, music breathing joy and comfort and gladness for us all to cherish through the long years to come.

You will want to play more of the beautiful compositions of Beethoven, and here you will find delightful minuets, sonatas, rondos, and country dances, all of them written by the great master.

RONDO
(TRACK 23)

MINUETTO
(TRACK 24)

ANDANTE
(TRACK 25)

SCHERZO
(TRACK 26)

ALBUMLEAF
"For Elise"
(TRACK 27)

ALLEGRETTO
(TRACK 28)

RONDO

VIVACE
(TRACK 30)

SONATA
(TRACK 31)

SONATA

SONATA
(TRACK 33)

THE END

CPSIA information can be obtained at www.ICGtesting.com
Printed in the USA
266666BV00005B/115-276/P